SONATINA FAVORITES

Selected and edited by
James Bastien

Bo

MW01011920

TO THE STUDENT

SONATINA FAVORITES, BOOK 3 provides representative literature at the advanced intermediate level. Great and lesser composers are represented. Themes are identified in this edition to aid in becoming aware of sonatina form.

Most sonatinas are student pieces designed to serve as models to study before playing more difficult sonatas later. In this regard, a sonatina is a *little sonata*.

PRACTICE SUGGESTIONS

1. Practice *hands separately* to establish the basic hand motions.
2. Practice in *sections*.
3. Practice *slowly* at first; keep a steady beat; gradually increase the tempo. A metronome may be used to help control the tempo.

MEMORY SUGGESTIONS

1. Analyze the form of each movement.
2. Learn each section of each movement from memory; be able to start at any section from memory.
3. Know the tonality (key) in each section of each movement. Analyze the harmony used in each movement.

CONTEST REMINDERS

Sonatinas are often used in auditions and contests. The examiner or judge will be observing these points:

1. correct notes and rhythm .
2. steady tempo
3. correct dynamics and phrasing (touch)
4. correct balance of melody and accompaniment
5. appropriate style and mood of each movement necessary for a convincing performance

CONTENTS

GWM GENERAL WORDS AND MUSIC COMPANY Neil A. Kjos Jr., Publisher   ISBN 0-8497-6096-8

Published by General Words and Music Co.

Distributed by Neil A. Kjos Music Company
4382 Jutland Drive, San Diego, California 92117

© 1977 General Words and Music Co., Park Ridge, Illinois

SONATINA FORM

The form of sonatinas varies: a sonatina may have one, two, or three short movements. These movements have contrasts in tempo and mood. Played as a whole, a sonatina has an overall plan making a complete piece.

The **first movement** of a sonatina usually has two main themes:
1. first theme
2. second theme

First movements of longer sonatinas often have this form:
1. EXPOSITION SECTION (statement of themes)
   a) first theme
   b) second theme (usually in a contrasting key)
   c) closing theme (optional)
2. DEVELOPMENT SECTION
   (Usually previous themes are presented in new keys; however, sometimes a new theme is used.)
3. RECAPITULATION SECTION (restatement of themes)
   a) first theme (sometimes omitted if used extensively in the development section)
   b) second theme
   c) closing theme (optional)

The **second movement** of a sonatina usually is written in *three-part song form:*
1. first theme (part 1)
2. second theme (part 2)
3. first theme (repeat of part 1)

The **third movement** of a sonatina is often written in *rondo form:*
1. first theme (section A)
2. second theme (section B)
3. third theme (section C — optional)
4. first theme (section A)
5. second theme (section B)
6. coda (optional)

SONATINA Op. 36, No. 3

Muzio Clementi

> **Muzio Clementi (1752-1832)** was a famous Italian pianist, composer, and teacher. In 1781 he and Mozart had a contest to determine which one was the better pianist. Although no winner was announced, Clementi was thought to have a better technique, but the audience felt that Mozart was a finer musician. Clementi wrote *The Art of Playing on the Piano-Forte* which he used with his beginning students. Chopin also used this book with his students. In addition to his teaching, composing, and performing, Clementi established a successful piano factory and a publishing company.

Spiritoso

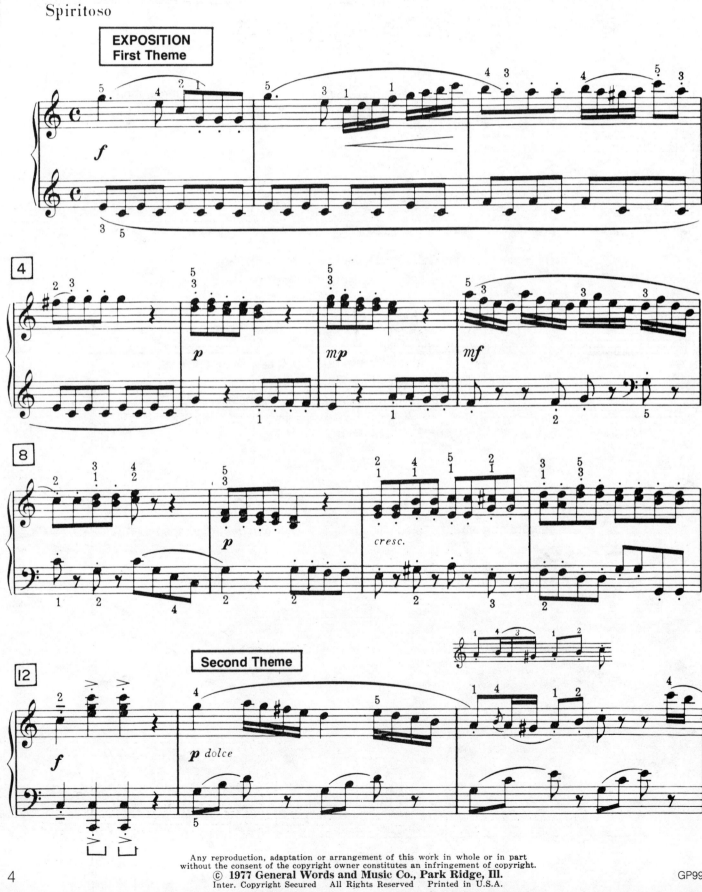

GP99

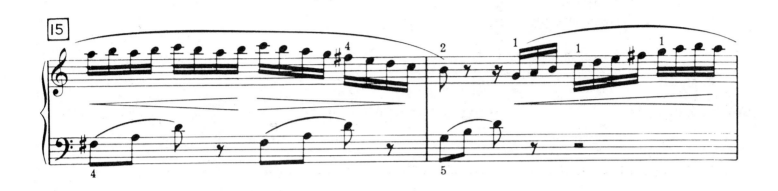

DEVELOPMENT
First Theme (Inverted)

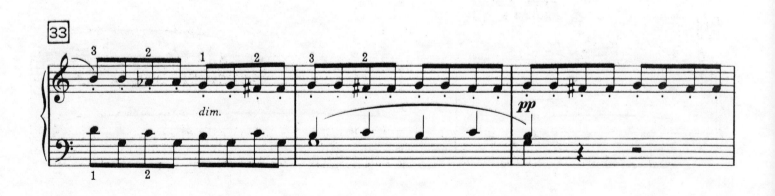

RECAPITULATION
First Theme

Second Theme

8

Un poco adagio

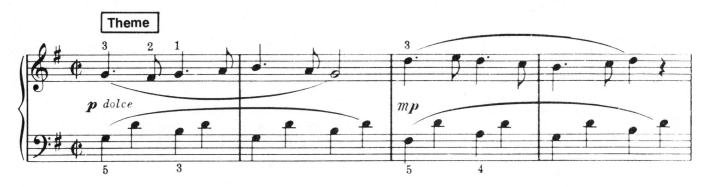

Allegro

First Theme

SONATINA Op. 55, No. 1

Friedrich Kuhlau

Friedrich Kuhlau (1786-1832), a German composer, lost an eye in a childhood accident. He studied the piano during his recovery. Kuhlau lived most of his adult life in Denmark where he played the flute in the King's Band. He wrote numerous flute compositions, violin sonatas, two piano concertos, piano sonatas, and many sonatinas which are played by students the world over.

Second Theme

Closing Theme

Rondo

Vivace

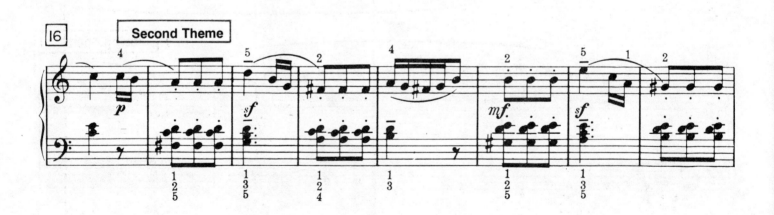

First Theme

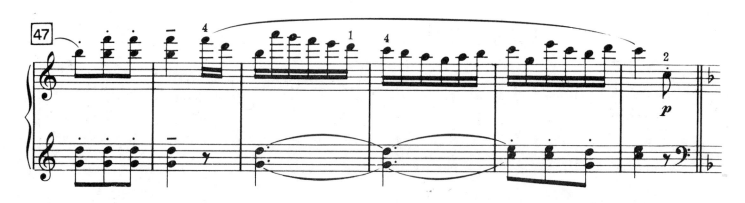

Transition

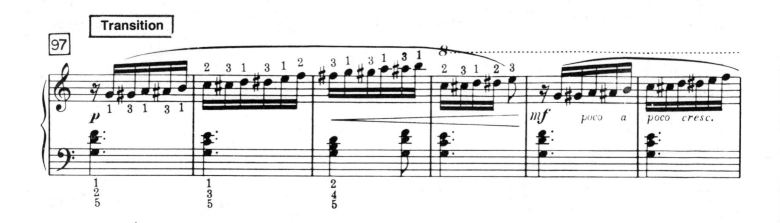

Coda

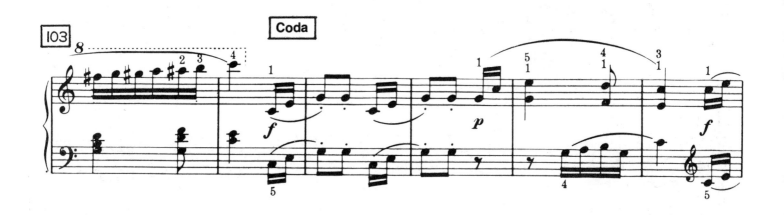

SONATINA Op. 55, No. 3

Friedrich Kuhlau

GP99

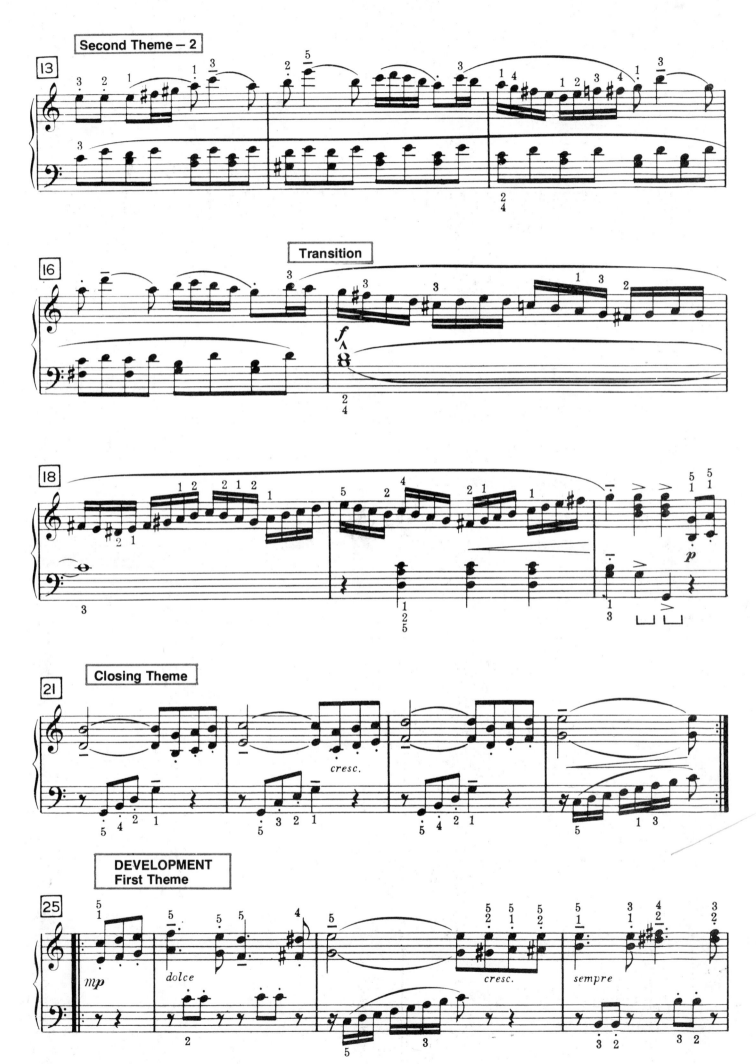

RECAPITULATION
Second Theme — 1

Second Theme — 2

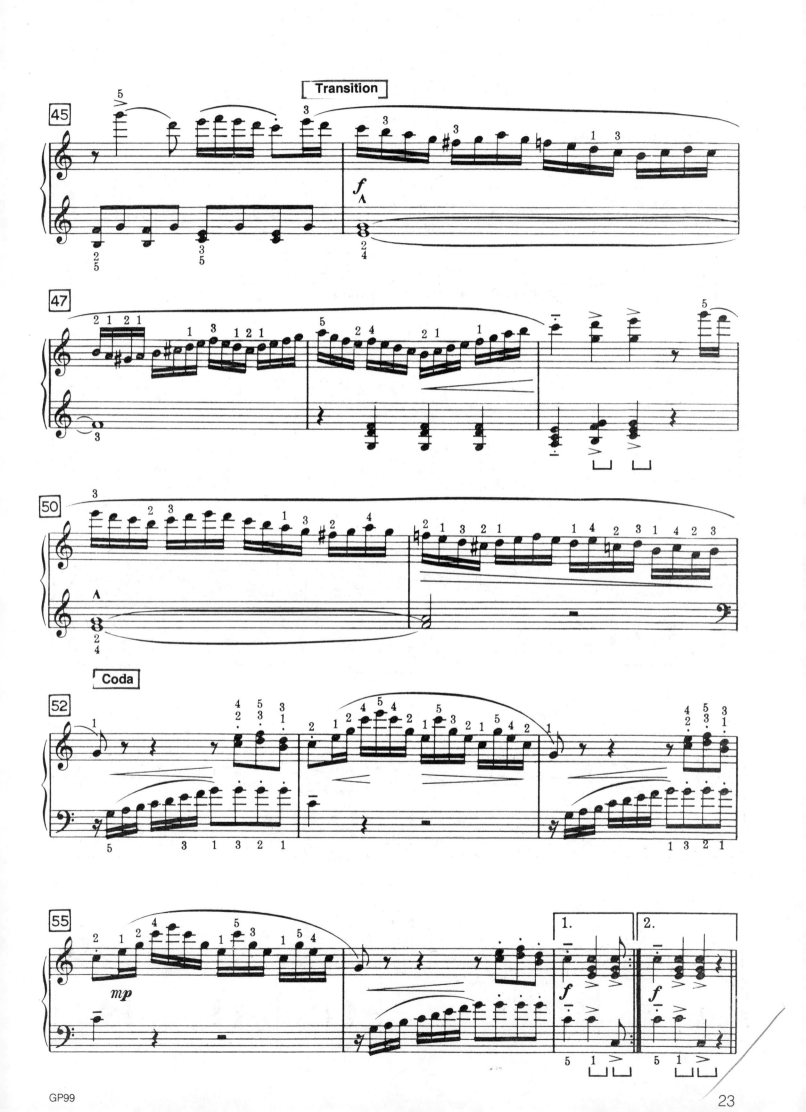

Rondo

Allegretto grazioso

First Theme

GP99

SONATINA IN CONTEMPORARY STYLE

James Bastien

DEVELOPMENT
First Theme

II
Canzonetta

Con moto (♩.=60)

First Theme

con moto espressione

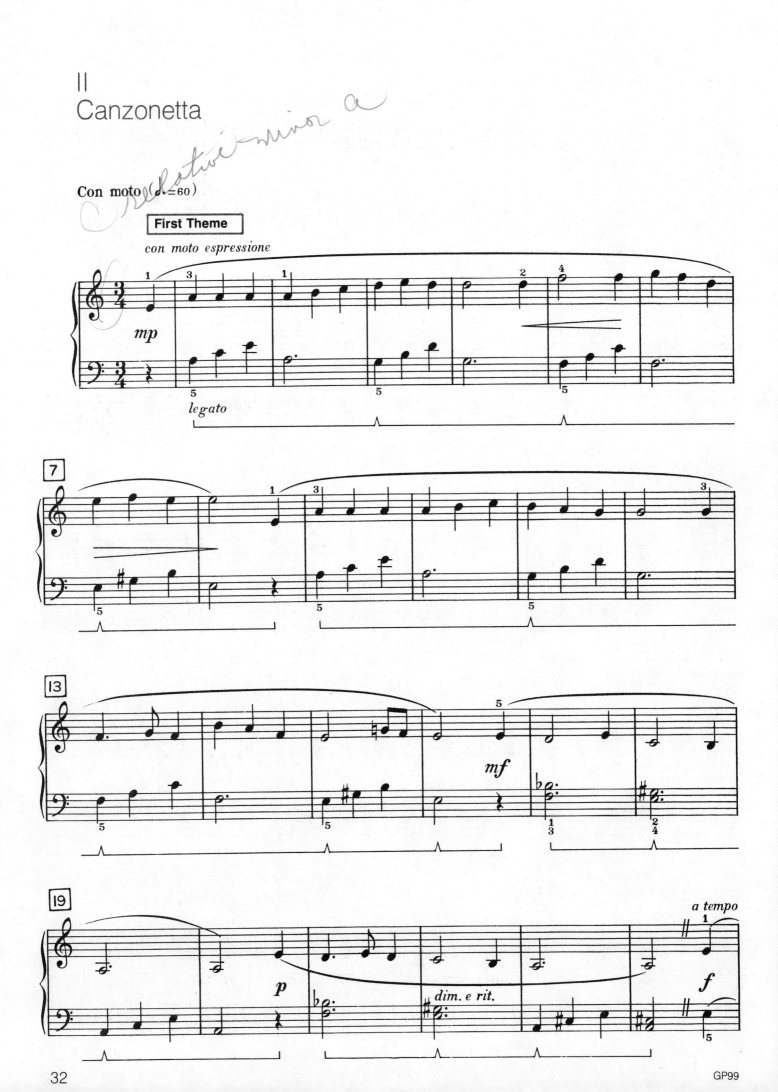

First Theme

34

III
Tarantella

Vivace ($\text{♩.} = 132$)

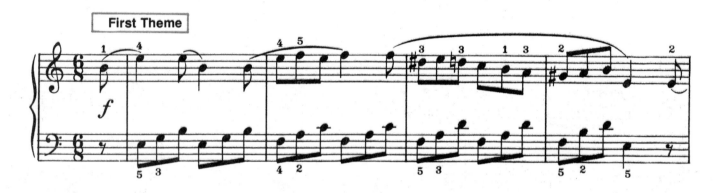

First Theme